CASH BREAKDOWN

forms by showversation

Stay *focused*

"It's not how much money you make, but how much money you keep, how hard it works for you, and how many generations you keep it for."

Cash Breakdown

Date:

CASH ENVELOPES/SINKING FUNDS

CATEGORY	AMOUNT	BANKING WITHDRAWAL DENOMINATIONS					
		$1	$5	$10	$20	$50	$100
		Total Number of Each Bill					
TOTAL	$						

INCOME

INCOME SOURCE	AMOUNT	Salary/Wages	Investment	Business	Side-Hustle
Rollover from previous week		☐	☐	☐	☐
		☐	☐	☐	☐
		☐	☐	☐	☐
		☐	☐	☐	☐
		☐	☐	☐	☐
		☐	☐	☐	☐
		☐	☐	☐	☐
		☐	☐	☐	☐
		☐	☐	☐	☐
Total Income	$				
minus - Total Cash Envelopes	$				
Remaining Balance	$				

Double Check It! Calculations

Cash Breakdown

Date:

CASH ENVELOPES/SINKING FUNDS

CATEGORY	AMOUNT	BANKING WITHDRAWAL DENOMINATIONS					
		$1	$5	$10	$20	$50	$100
		Total Number of Each Bill					
TOTAL	$						

INCOME

INCOME SOURCE	AMOUNT	Salary/Wages	Investment	Business	Side-Hustle
Rollover from previous week		☐	☐	☐	☐
		☐	☐	☐	☐
		☐	☐	☐	☐
		☐	☐	☐	☐
		☐	☐	☐	☐
		☐	☐	☐	☐
		☐	☐	☐	☐
		☐	☐	☐	☐
		☐	☐	☐	☐
Total Income	$				
minus - Total Cash Envelopes	$				
Remaining Balance	$				

Double Check It! Calculations

Cash Breakdown

Date:

CASH ENVELOPES/SINKING FUNDS

CATEGORY	AMOUNT	BANKING WITHDRAWAL DENOMINATIONS					
		$1	$5	$10	$20	$50	$100
		Total Number of Each Bill					
TOTAL	$						

INCOME

INCOME SOURCE	AMOUNT	Salary/Wages	Investment	Business	Side-Hustle
Rollover from previous week		☐	☐	☐	☐
		☐	☐	☐	☐
		☐	☐	☐	☐
		☐	☐	☐	☐
		☐	☐	☐	☐
		☐	☐	☐	☐
		☐	☐	☐	☐
		☐	☐	☐	☐
		☐	☐	☐	☐
Total Income	$				
minus - Total Cash Envelopes	$				
Remaining Balance	$				

Double Check It! Calculations

Cash Breakdown

Date:

CASH ENVELOPES/SINKING FUNDS

CATEGORY	AMOUNT	BANKING WITHDRAWAL DENOMINATIONS					
		$1	$5	$10	$20	$50	$100
		Total Number of Each Bill					
TOTAL	$						

INCOME

INCOME SOURCE	AMOUNT	Salary/Wages	Investment	Business	Side-Hustle
Rollover from previous week		☐	☐	☐	☐
		☐	☐	☐	☐
		☐	☐	☐	☐
		☐	☐	☐	☐
		☐	☐	☐	☐
		☐	☐	☐	☐
		☐	☐	☐	☐
		☐	☐	☐	☐
		☐	☐	☐	☐
Total Income	$				
minus - Total Cash Envelopes	$				
Remaining Balance	$				

Double Check It! Calculations

Cash Breakdown

Date:

CASH ENVELOPES/SINKING FUNDS

CATEGORY	AMOUNT	BANKING WITHDRAWAL DENOMINATIONS					
		$1	$5	$10	$20	$50	$100
		Total Number of Each Bill					
TOTAL	$						

INCOME

INCOME SOURCE	AMOUNT	Salary/Wages	Investment	Business	Side-Hustle
Rollover from previous week		☐	☐	☐	☐
		☐	☐	☐	☐
		☐	☐	☐	☐
		☐	☐	☐	☐
		☐	☐	☐	☐
		☐	☐	☐	☐
		☐	☐	☐	☐
		☐	☐	☐	☐
		☐	☐	☐	☐
Total Income	$				
minus - Total Cash Envelopes	$				
Remaining Balance	$				

Double Check It! Calculations

Cash Breakdown

Date:

CASH ENVELOPES/SINKING FUNDS

CATEGORY	AMOUNT	BANKING WITHDRAWAL DENOMINATIONS					
		$1	$5	$10	$20	$50	$100
		Total Number of Each Bill					
TOTAL	$						

INCOME

INCOME SOURCE	AMOUNT	Salary/Wages	Investment	Business	Side-Hustle
Rollover from previous week		☐	☐	☐	☐
		☐	☐	☐	☐
		☐	☐	☐	☐
		☐	☐	☐	☐
		☐	☐	☐	☐
		☐	☐	☐	☐
		☐	☐	☐	☐
		☐	☐	☐	☐
		☐	☐	☐	☐
Total Income	$				
minus - Total Cash Envelopes	$				
Remaining Balance	$				

Double Check It! Calculations

Cash Breakdown

Date:

CASH ENVELOPES/SINKING FUNDS

CATEGORY	AMOUNT	BANKING WITHDRAWAL DENOMINATIONS					
		$1	$5	$10	$20	$50	$100
		Total Number of Each Bill					
TOTAL	$						

INCOME

INCOME SOURCE	AMOUNT	Salary/Wages	Investment	Business	Side-Hustle
Rollover from previous week		☐	☐	☐	☐
		☐	☐	☐	☐
		☐	☐	☐	☐
		☐	☐	☐	☐
		☐	☐	☐	☐
		☐	☐	☐	☐
		☐	☐	☐	☐
		☐	☐	☐	☐
		☐	☐	☐	☐
Total Income	$				
minus - Total Cash Envelopes	$				
Remaining Balance	$				

Double Check It! Calculations

Cash Breakdown

Date:

CASH ENVELOPES/SINKING FUNDS

CATEGORY	AMOUNT	BANKING WITHDRAWAL DENOMINATIONS					
		$1	$5	$10	$20	$50	$100
		Total Number of Each Bill					
TOTAL	$						

INCOME

INCOME SOURCE	AMOUNT	Salary/Wages	Investment	Business	Side-Hustle
Rollover from previous week		☐	☐	☐	☐
		☐	☐	☐	☐
		☐	☐	☐	☐
		☐	☐	☐	☐
		☐	☐	☐	☐
		☐	☐	☐	☐
		☐	☐	☐	☐
		☐	☐	☐	☐
		☐	☐	☐	☐
Total Income	$				
minus - Total Cash Envelopes	$				
Remaining Balance	$				

Double Check It! Calculations

Cash Breakdown

Date:

CASH ENVELOPES/SINKING FUNDS

CATEGORY	AMOUNT	BANKING WITHDRAWAL DENOMINATIONS					
		$1	$5	$10	$20	$50	$100
		Total Number of Each Bill					
TOTAL	$						

INCOME

INCOME SOURCE	AMOUNT	Salary/Wages	Investment	Business	Side-Hustle
Rollover from previous week		☐	☐	☐	☐
		☐	☐	☐	☐
		☐	☐	☐	☐
		☐	☐	☐	☐
		☐	☐	☐	☐
		☐	☐	☐	☐
		☐	☐	☐	☐
		☐	☐	☐	☐
		☐	☐	☐	☐
Total Income	$				
minus - Total Cash Envelopes	$				
Remaining Balance	$				

Double Check It! Calculations

Cash Breakdown

Date:

CASH ENVELOPES/SINKING FUNDS

CATEGORY	AMOUNT	BANKING WITHDRAWAL DENOMINATIONS					
		$1	$5	$10	$20	$50	$100
		Total Number of Each Bill					
TOTAL	$						

INCOME

INCOME SOURCE	AMOUNT	Salary/Wages	Investment	Business	Side-Hustle
Rollover from previous week		☐	☐	☐	☐
		☐	☐	☐	☐
		☐	☐	☐	☐
		☐	☐	☐	☐
		☐	☐	☐	☐
		☐	☐	☐	☐
		☐	☐	☐	☐
		☐	☐	☐	☐
		☐	☐	☐	☐
Total Income	$				
minus - Total Cash Envelopes	$				
Remaining Balance	$				

Double Check It! Calculations

Cash Breakdown

Date:

CASH ENVELOPES/SINKING FUNDS

CATEGORY	AMOUNT	BANKING WITHDRAWAL DENOMINATIONS					
		$1	$5	$10	$20	$50	$100
		Total Number of Each Bill					
TOTAL	$						

INCOME

INCOME SOURCE	AMOUNT	Salary/Wages	Investment	Business	Side-Hustle
Rollover from previous week		☐	☐	☐	☐
		☐	☐	☐	☐
		☐	☐	☐	☐
		☐	☐	☐	☐
		☐	☐	☐	☐
		☐	☐	☐	☐
		☐	☐	☐	☐
		☐	☐	☐	☐
		☐	☐	☐	☐
Total Income	$				
minus - Total Cash Envelopes	$				
Remaining Balance	$				

Double Check It! Calculations

Cash Breakdown

Date:

CASH ENVELOPES/SINKING FUNDS

CATEGORY	AMOUNT	BANKING WITHDRAWAL DENOMINATIONS					
		$1	$5	$10	$20	$50	$100
		Total Number of Each Bill					
TOTAL	$						

INCOME

INCOME SOURCE	AMOUNT	Salary/Wages	Investment	Business	Side-Hustle
Rollover from previous week		☐	☐	☐	☐
		☐	☐	☐	☐
		☐	☐	☐	☐
		☐	☐	☐	☐
		☐	☐	☐	☐
		☐	☐	☐	☐
		☐	☐	☐	☐
		☐	☐	☐	☐
		☐	☐	☐	☐
Total Income	$				
minus - Total Cash Envelopes	$				
Remaining Balance	$				

Double Check It! Calculations

Cash Breakdown

Date:

CASH ENVELOPES/SINKING FUNDS

CATEGORY	AMOUNT	BANKING WITHDRAWAL DENOMINATIONS					
		$1	$5	$10	$20	$50	$100
		Total Number of Each Bill					
TOTAL	$						

INCOME

INCOME SOURCE	AMOUNT	Salary/Wages	Investment	Business	Side-Hustle
Rollover from previous week		☐	☐	☐	☐
		☐	☐	☐	☐
		☐	☐	☐	☐
		☐	☐	☐	☐
		☐	☐	☐	☐
		☐	☐	☐	☐
		☐	☐	☐	☐
		☐	☐	☐	☐
		☐	☐	☐	☐
Total Income	$				
minus - Total Cash Envelopes	$				
Remaining Balance	$				

Double Check It! Calculations

Cash Breakdown

Date:

CASH ENVELOPES/SINKING FUNDS

CATEGORY	AMOUNT	BANKING WITHDRAWAL DENOMINATIONS					
		$1	$5	$10	$20	$50	$100
		Total Number of Each Bill					
TOTAL	$						

INCOME

INCOME SOURCE	AMOUNT	Salary/Wages	Investment	Business	Side-Hustle
Rollover from previous week		☐	☐	☐	☐
		☐	☐	☐	☐
		☐	☐	☐	☐
		☐	☐	☐	☐
		☐	☐	☐	☐
		☐	☐	☐	☐
		☐	☐	☐	☐
		☐	☐	☐	☐
		☐	☐	☐	☐
Total Income	$				
minus - Total Cash Envelopes	$				
Remaining Balance	$				

Double Check It! Calculations

Cash Breakdown

Date:

CASH ENVELOPES/SINKING FUNDS

CATEGORY	AMOUNT	BANKING WITHDRAWAL DENOMINATIONS					
		$1	$5	$10	$20	$50	$100
		Total Number of Each Bill					
TOTAL	$						

INCOME

INCOME SOURCE	AMOUNT	Salary/Wages	Investment	Business	Side-Hustle
Rollover from previous week		☐	☐	☐	☐
		☐	☐	☐	☐
		☐	☐	☐	☐
		☐	☐	☐	☐
		☐	☐	☐	☐
		☐	☐	☐	☐
		☐	☐	☐	☐
		☐	☐	☐	☐
		☐	☐	☐	☐
Total Income	$				
minus - Total Cash Envelopes	$				
Remaining Balance	$				

Double Check It! Calculations

Cash Breakdown

Date:

CASH ENVELOPES/SINKING FUNDS

CATEGORY	AMOUNT	BANKING WITHDRAWAL DENOMINATIONS					
		$1	$5	$10	$20	$50	$100
		Total Number of Each Bill					
TOTAL	$						

INCOME

INCOME SOURCE	AMOUNT	Salary/Wages	Investment	Business	Side-Hustle
Rollover from previous week		☐	☐	☐	☐
		☐	☐	☐	☐
		☐	☐	☐	☐
		☐	☐	☐	☐
		☐	☐	☐	☐
		☐	☐	☐	☐
		☐	☐	☐	☐
		☐	☐	☐	☐
		☐	☐	☐	☐
Total Income	$				
minus - Total Cash Envelopes	$				
Remaining Balance	$				

Double Check It! Calculations

Cash Breakdown

Date:

CASH ENVELOPES/SINKING FUNDS

CATEGORY	AMOUNT	BANKING WITHDRAWAL DENOMINATIONS					
		$1	$5	$10	$20	$50	$100
		Total Number of Each Bill					
TOTAL	$						

INCOME

INCOME SOURCE	AMOUNT	Salary/Wages	Investment	Business	Side-Hustle
Rollover from previous week		☐	☐	☐	☐
		☐	☐	☐	☐
		☐	☐	☐	☐
		☐	☐	☐	☐
		☐	☐	☐	☐
		☐	☐	☐	☐
		☐	☐	☐	☐
		☐	☐	☐	☐
		☐	☐	☐	☐
Total Income	$				
minus - Total Cash Envelopes	$				
Remaining Balance	$				

Double Check It! Calculations

Cash Breakdown

Date:

CASH ENVELOPES/SINKING FUNDS

CATEGORY	AMOUNT	BANKING WITHDRAWAL DENOMINATIONS					
		$1	$5	$10	$20	$50	$100
		Total Number of Each Bill					
TOTAL	$						

INCOME

INCOME SOURCE	AMOUNT	Salary/Wages	Investment	Business	Side-Hustle
Rollover from previous week		☐	☐	☐	☐
		☐	☐	☐	☐
		☐	☐	☐	☐
		☐	☐	☐	☐
		☐	☐	☐	☐
		☐	☐	☐	☐
		☐	☐	☐	☐
		☐	☐	☐	☐
		☐	☐	☐	☐
Total Income	$				
minus - Total Cash Envelopes	$				
Remaining Balance	$				

Double Check It! Calculations

Cash Breakdown

Date:

CASH ENVELOPES/SINKING FUNDS

CATEGORY	AMOUNT	BANKING WITHDRAWAL DENOMINATIONS					
		$1	$5	$10	$20	$50	$100
		Total Number of Each Bill					
TOTAL	$						

INCOME

INCOME SOURCE	AMOUNT	Salary/Wages	Investment	Business	Side-Hustle
Rollover from previous week		☐	☐	☐	☐
		☐	☐	☐	☐
		☐	☐	☐	☐
		☐	☐	☐	☐
		☐	☐	☐	☐
		☐	☐	☐	☐
		☐	☐	☐	☐
		☐	☐	☐	☐
		☐	☐	☐	☐
Total Income	$				
minus - Total Cash Envelopes	$				
Remaining Balance	$				

Double Check It! Calculations

Cash Breakdown

Date:

CASH ENVELOPES/SINKING FUNDS

CATEGORY	AMOUNT	BANKING WITHDRAWAL DENOMINATIONS					
		$1	$5	$10	$20	$50	$100
		Total Number of Each Bill					
TOTAL	$						

INCOME

INCOME SOURCE	AMOUNT	Salary/Wages	Investment	Business	Side-Hustle
Rollover from previous week		☐	☐	☐	☐
		☐	☐	☐	☐
		☐	☐	☐	☐
		☐	☐	☐	☐
		☐	☐	☐	☐
		☐	☐	☐	☐
		☐	☐	☐	☐
		☐	☐	☐	☐
		☐	☐	☐	☐
Total Income	$				
minus - Total Cash Envelopes	$				
Remaining Balance	$				

Double Check It! Calculations

Cash Breakdown

Date:

CASH ENVELOPES/SINKING FUNDS

CATEGORY	AMOUNT	BANKING WITHDRAWAL DENOMINATIONS					
		$1	$5	$10	$20	$50	$100
		Total Number of Each Bill					
TOTAL	$						

INCOME

INCOME SOURCE	AMOUNT	Salary/Wages	Investment	Business	Side-Hustle
Rollover from previous week		☐	☐	☐	☐
		☐	☐	☐	☐
		☐	☐	☐	☐
		☐	☐	☐	☐
		☐	☐	☐	☐
		☐	☐	☐	☐
		☐	☐	☐	☐
		☐	☐	☐	☐
		☐	☐	☐	☐
Total Income	$				
minus - Total Cash Envelopes	$				
Remaining Balance	$				

Double Check It! Calculations

Cash Breakdown

Date:

CASH ENVELOPES/SINKING FUNDS

CATEGORY	AMOUNT	BANKING WITHDRAWAL DENOMINATIONS					
		$1	$5	$10	$20	$50	$100
		Total Number of Each Bill					
TOTAL	$						

INCOME

INCOME SOURCE	AMOUNT	Salary/Wages	Investment	Business	Side-Hustle
Rollover from previous week		☐	☐	☐	☐
		☐	☐	☐	☐
		☐	☐	☐	☐
		☐	☐	☐	☐
		☐	☐	☐	☐
		☐	☐	☐	☐
		☐	☐	☐	☐
		☐	☐	☐	☐
		☐	☐	☐	☐

Total Income	$
minus - Total Cash Envelopes	$
Remaining Balance	$

Double Check It! Calculations

Cash Breakdown

Date:

CASH ENVELOPES/SINKING FUNDS

CATEGORY	AMOUNT	BANKING WITHDRAWAL DENOMINATIONS					
		$1	$5	$10	$20	$50	$100
		Total Number of Each Bill					
TOTAL	$						

INCOME

INCOME SOURCE	AMOUNT	Salary/Wages	Investment	Business	Side-Hustle
Rollover from previous week		☐	☐	☐	☐
		☐	☐	☐	☐
		☐	☐	☐	☐
		☐	☐	☐	☐
		☐	☐	☐	☐
		☐	☐	☐	☐
		☐	☐	☐	☐
		☐	☐	☐	☐
		☐	☐	☐	☐
Total Income	$				
minus - Total Cash Envelopes	$				
Remaining Balance	$				

Double Check It! Calculations

Cash Breakdown

Date:

CASH ENVELOPES/SINKING FUNDS

CATEGORY	AMOUNT	BANKING WITHDRAWAL DENOMINATIONS					
		$1	$5	$10	$20	$50	$100
		Total Number of Each Bill					
TOTAL	$						

INCOME

INCOME SOURCE	AMOUNT	Salary/Wages	Investment	Business	Side-Hustle
Rollover from previous week		☐	☐	☐	☐
		☐	☐	☐	☐
		☐	☐	☐	☐
		☐	☐	☐	☐
		☐	☐	☐	☐
		☐	☐	☐	☐
		☐	☐	☐	☐
		☐	☐	☐	☐
		☐	☐	☐	☐
Total Income	$				
minus - Total Cash Envelopes	$				
Remaining Balance	$				

Double Check It! Calculations

Cash Breakdown

Date:

CASH ENVELOPES/SINKING FUNDS

CATEGORY	AMOUNT	BANKING WITHDRAWAL DENOMINATIONS					
		$1	$5	$10	$20	$50	$100
		Total Number of Each Bill					
TOTAL	$						

INCOME

INCOME SOURCE	AMOUNT	Salary/Wages	Investment	Business	Side-Hustle
Rollover from previous week		☐	☐	☐	☐
		☐	☐	☐	☐
		☐	☐	☐	☐
		☐	☐	☐	☐
		☐	☐	☐	☐
		☐	☐	☐	☐
		☐	☐	☐	☐
		☐	☐	☐	☐
		☐	☐	☐	☐
Total Income	$				
minus - Total Cash Envelopes	$				
Remaining Balance	$				

Double Check It! Calculations

Cash Breakdown

Date:

CASH ENVELOPES/SINKING FUNDS

CATEGORY	AMOUNT	BANKING WITHDRAWAL DENOMINATIONS					
		$1	$5	$10	$20	$50	$100
		Total Number of Each Bill					
TOTAL	$						

INCOME

INCOME SOURCE	AMOUNT	Salary/Wages	Investment	Business	Side-Hustle
Rollover from previous week		☐	☐	☐	☐
		☐	☐	☐	☐
		☐	☐	☐	☐
		☐	☐	☐	☐
		☐	☐	☐	☐
		☐	☐	☐	☐
		☐	☐	☐	☐
		☐	☐	☐	☐
		☐	☐	☐	☐
Total Income	$				
minus - Total Cash Envelopes	$				
Remaining Balance	$				

Double Check It! Calculations

Cash Breakdown

Date:

CASH ENVELOPES/SINKING FUNDS

CATEGORY	AMOUNT	BANKING WITHDRAWAL DENOMINATIONS					
		$1	$5	$10	$20	$50	$100
		Total Number of Each Bill					
TOTAL	$						

INCOME

INCOME SOURCE	AMOUNT	Salary/Wages	Investment	Business	Side-Hustle
Rollover from previous week		☐	☐	☐	☐
		☐	☐	☐	☐
		☐	☐	☐	☐
		☐	☐	☐	☐
		☐	☐	☐	☐
		☐	☐	☐	☐
		☐	☐	☐	☐
		☐	☐	☐	☐
		☐	☐	☐	☐
Total Income	$				
minus - Total Cash Envelopes	$				
Remaining Balance	$				

Double Check It! Calculations

Cash Breakdown

Date:

CASH ENVELOPES/SINKING FUNDS

CATEGORY	AMOUNT	BANKING WITHDRAWAL DENOMINATIONS					
		$1	$5	$10	$20	$50	$100
		Total Number of Each Bill					
TOTAL	$						

INCOME

INCOME SOURCE	AMOUNT	Salary/Wages	Investment	Business	Side-Hustle
Rollover from previous week		☐	☐	☐	☐
		☐	☐	☐	☐
		☐	☐	☐	☐
		☐	☐	☐	☐
		☐	☐	☐	☐
		☐	☐	☐	☐
		☐	☐	☐	☐
		☐	☐	☐	☐
		☐	☐	☐	☐
Total Income	$				
minus - Total Cash Envelopes	$				
Remaining Balance	$				

Double Check It! Calculations

Cash Breakdown

Date:

CASH ENVELOPES/SINKING FUNDS

CATEGORY	AMOUNT	BANKING WITHDRAWAL DENOMINATIONS					
		$1	$5	$10	$20	$50	$100
		Total Number of Each Bill					
TOTAL	$						

INCOME

INCOME SOURCE	AMOUNT	Salary/Wages	Investment	Business	Side-Hustle
Rollover from previous week		☐	☐	☐	☐
		☐	☐	☐	☐
		☐	☐	☐	☐
		☐	☐	☐	☐
		☐	☐	☐	☐
		☐	☐	☐	☐
		☐	☐	☐	☐
		☐	☐	☐	☐
		☐	☐	☐	☐
Total Income	$				
minus - Total Cash Envelopes	$				
Remaining Balance	$				

Double Check It! Calculations

Cash Breakdown

Date:

CASH ENVELOPES/SINKING FUNDS

CATEGORY	AMOUNT	BANKING WITHDRAWAL DENOMINATIONS					
		$1	$5	$10	$20	$50	$100
		Total Number of Each Bill					
TOTAL	$						

INCOME

INCOME SOURCE	AMOUNT	Salary/Wages	Investment	Business	Side-Hustle
Rollover from previous week		☐	☐	☐	☐
		☐	☐	☐	☐
		☐	☐	☐	☐
		☐	☐	☐	☐
		☐	☐	☐	☐
		☐	☐	☐	☐
		☐	☐	☐	☐
		☐	☐	☐	☐
		☐	☐	☐	☐
Total Income	$				
minus - Total Cash Envelopes	$				
Remaining Balance	$				

Double Check It! Calculations

Cash Breakdown

Date:

CASH ENVELOPES/SINKING FUNDS

CATEGORY	AMOUNT	BANKING WITHDRAWAL DENOMINATIONS					
		$1	$5	$10	$20	$50	$100
		Total Number of Each Bill					
TOTAL	$						

INCOME

INCOME SOURCE	AMOUNT	Salary/Wages	Investment	Business	Side-Hustle
Rollover from previous week		☐	☐	☐	☐
		☐	☐	☐	☐
		☐	☐	☐	☐
		☐	☐	☐	☐
		☐	☐	☐	☐
		☐	☐	☐	☐
		☐	☐	☐	☐
		☐	☐	☐	☐
		☐	☐	☐	☐
Total Income	$				
minus - Total Cash Envelopes	$				
Remaining Balance	$				

Double Check It! Calculations

Cash Breakdown

Date:

CASH ENVELOPES/SINKING FUNDS

CATEGORY	AMOUNT	BANKING WITHDRAWAL DENOMINATIONS					
		$1	$5	$10	$20	$50	$100
		Total Number of Each Bill					
TOTAL	$						

INCOME

INCOME SOURCE	AMOUNT	Salary/Wages	Investment	Business	Side-Hustle
Rollover from previous week		☐	☐	☐	☐
		☐	☐	☐	☐
		☐	☐	☐	☐
		☐	☐	☐	☐
		☐	☐	☐	☐
		☐	☐	☐	☐
		☐	☐	☐	☐
		☐	☐	☐	☐
		☐	☐	☐	☐
Total Income	$				
minus - Total Cash Envelopes	$				
Remaining Balance	$				

Double Check It! Calculations

Cash Breakdown

Date:

CASH ENVELOPES/SINKING FUNDS

CATEGORY	AMOUNT	BANKING WITHDRAWAL DENOMINATIONS					
		$1	$5	$10	$20	$50	$100
		Total Number of Each Bill					
TOTAL	$						

INCOME

INCOME SOURCE	AMOUNT	Salary/Wages	Investment	Business	Side-Hustle
Rollover from previous week		☐	☐	☐	☐
		☐	☐	☐	☐
		☐	☐	☐	☐
		☐	☐	☐	☐
		☐	☐	☐	☐
		☐	☐	☐	☐
		☐	☐	☐	☐
		☐	☐	☐	☐
		☐	☐	☐	☐
Total Income	$				
minus - Total Cash Envelopes	$				
Remaining Balance	$				

Double Check It! Calculations

Cash Breakdown

Date:

CASH ENVELOPES/SINKING FUNDS

CATEGORY	AMOUNT	BANKING WITHDRAWAL DENOMINATIONS					
		$1	$5	$10	$20	$50	$100
		Total Number of Each Bill					
TOTAL	$						

INCOME

INCOME SOURCE	AMOUNT	Salary/Wages	Investment	Business	Side-Hustle
Rollover from previous week		☐	☐	☐	☐
		☐	☐	☐	☐
		☐	☐	☐	☐
		☐	☐	☐	☐
		☐	☐	☐	☐
		☐	☐	☐	☐
		☐	☐	☐	☐
		☐	☐	☐	☐
		☐	☐	☐	☐
Total Income	$				
minus - Total Cash Envelopes	$				
Remaining Balance	$				

Double Check It! Calculations

Cash Breakdown

Date:

CASH ENVELOPES/SINKING FUNDS

CATEGORY	AMOUNT	BANKING WITHDRAWAL DENOMINATIONS					
		$1	$5	$10	$20	$50	$100
		Total Number of Each Bill					
TOTAL	$						

INCOME

INCOME SOURCE	AMOUNT	Salary/Wages	Investment	Business	Side-Hustle
Rollover from previous week		☐	☐	☐	☐
		☐	☐	☐	☐
		☐	☐	☐	☐
		☐	☐	☐	☐
		☐	☐	☐	☐
		☐	☐	☐	☐
		☐	☐	☐	☐
		☐	☐	☐	☐
		☐	☐	☐	☐
Total Income	$				
minus - Total Cash Envelopes	$				
Remaining Balance	$				

Double Check It! Calculations

Cash Breakdown

Date:

CASH ENVELOPES/SINKING FUNDS

CATEGORY	AMOUNT	BANKING WITHDRAWAL DENOMINATIONS					
		$1	$5	$10	$20	$50	$100
		Total Number of Each Bill					
TOTAL	$						

INCOME

INCOME SOURCE	AMOUNT	Salary/Wages	Investment	Business	Side-Hustle
Rollover from previous week		☐	☐	☐	☐
		☐	☐	☐	☐
		☐	☐	☐	☐
		☐	☐	☐	☐
		☐	☐	☐	☐
		☐	☐	☐	☐
		☐	☐	☐	☐
		☐	☐	☐	☐
		☐	☐	☐	☐
Total Income	$				
minus - Total Cash Envelopes	$				
Remaining Balance	$				

Double Check It! Calculations

Cash Breakdown

Date:

CASH ENVELOPES/SINKING FUNDS

CATEGORY	AMOUNT	BANKING WITHDRAWAL DENOMINATIONS					
		$1	$5	$10	$20	$50	$100
		Total Number of Each Bill					
TOTAL	$						

INCOME

INCOME SOURCE	AMOUNT	Salary/Wages	Investment	Business	Side-Hustle
Rollover from previous week		☐	☐	☐	☐
		☐	☐	☐	☐
		☐	☐	☐	☐
		☐	☐	☐	☐
		☐	☐	☐	☐
		☐	☐	☐	☐
		☐	☐	☐	☐
		☐	☐	☐	☐
		☐	☐	☐	☐
Total Income	$				
minus - Total Cash Envelopes	$				
Remaining Balance	$				

Double Check It! Calculations

Cash Breakdown

Date:

CASH ENVELOPES/SINKING FUNDS

CATEGORY	AMOUNT	BANKING WITHDRAWAL DENOMINATIONS					
		$1	$5	$10	$20	$50	$100
		Total Number of Each Bill					
TOTAL	$						

INCOME

INCOME SOURCE	AMOUNT	Salary/Wages	Investment	Business	Side-Hustle
Rollover from previous week		☐	☐	☐	☐
		☐	☐	☐	☐
		☐	☐	☐	☐
		☐	☐	☐	☐
		☐	☐	☐	☐
		☐	☐	☐	☐
		☐	☐	☐	☐
		☐	☐	☐	☐
		☐	☐	☐	☐
Total Income	$				
minus - Total Cash Envelopes	$				
Remaining Balance	$				

Double Check It! Calculations

Cash Breakdown

Date:

CASH ENVELOPES/SINKING FUNDS

CATEGORY	AMOUNT	BANKING WITHDRAWAL DENOMINATIONS					
		$1	$5	$10	$20	$50	$100
		Total Number of Each Bill					
TOTAL	$						

INCOME

INCOME SOURCE	AMOUNT	Salary/Wages	Investment	Business	Side-Hustle
Rollover from previous week		☐	☐	☐	☐
		☐	☐	☐	☐
		☐	☐	☐	☐
		☐	☐	☐	☐
		☐	☐	☐	☐
		☐	☐	☐	☐
		☐	☐	☐	☐
		☐	☐	☐	☐
		☐	☐	☐	☐
Total Income	$				
minus - Total Cash Envelopes	$				
Remaining Balance	$				

Double Check It! Calculations

Cash Breakdown

Date:

CASH ENVELOPES/SINKING FUNDS

CATEGORY	AMOUNT	BANKING WITHDRAWAL DENOMINATIONS					
		$1	$5	$10	$20	$50	$100
		Total Number of Each Bill					
TOTAL	$						

INCOME

INCOME SOURCE	AMOUNT	Salary/Wages	Investment	Business	Side-Hustle
Rollover from previous week		☐	☐	☐	☐
		☐	☐	☐	☐
		☐	☐	☐	☐
		☐	☐	☐	☐
		☐	☐	☐	☐
		☐	☐	☐	☐
		☐	☐	☐	☐
		☐	☐	☐	☐
		☐	☐	☐	☐
Total Income	$				
minus - Total Cash Envelopes	$				
Remaining Balance	$				

Double Check It! Calculations

Cash Breakdown

Date:

CASH ENVELOPES/SINKING FUNDS

CATEGORY	AMOUNT	BANKING WITHDRAWAL DENOMINATIONS					
		$1	$5	$10	$20	$50	$100
		Total Number of Each Bill					
TOTAL	$						

INCOME

INCOME SOURCE	AMOUNT	Salary/Wages	Investment	Business	Side-Hustle
Rollover from previous week		☐	☐	☐	☐
		☐	☐	☐	☐
		☐	☐	☐	☐
		☐	☐	☐	☐
		☐	☐	☐	☐
		☐	☐	☐	☐
		☐	☐	☐	☐
		☐	☐	☐	☐
		☐	☐	☐	☐
Total Income	$				
minus - Total Cash Envelopes	$				
Remaining Balance	$				

Double Check It! Calculations

Cash Breakdown

Date:

CASH ENVELOPES/SINKING FUNDS

CATEGORY	AMOUNT	BANKING WITHDRAWAL DENOMINATIONS					
		$1	$5	$10	$20	$50	$100
		Total Number of Each Bill					
TOTAL	$						

INCOME

INCOME SOURCE	AMOUNT	Salary/Wages	Investment	Business	Side-Hustle
Rollover from previous week		☐	☐	☐	☐
		☐	☐	☐	☐
		☐	☐	☐	☐
		☐	☐	☐	☐
		☐	☐	☐	☐
		☐	☐	☐	☐
		☐	☐	☐	☐
		☐	☐	☐	☐
		☐	☐	☐	☐
Total Income	$				
minus - Total Cash Envelopes	$				
Remaining Balance	$				

Double Check It! Calculations

Cash Breakdown

Date:

CASH ENVELOPES/SINKING FUNDS

CATEGORY	AMOUNT	BANKING WITHDRAWAL DENOMINATIONS					
		$1	$5	$10	$20	$50	$100
		Total Number of Each Bill					
TOTAL	$						

INCOME

INCOME SOURCE	AMOUNT	Salary/Wages	Investment	Business	Side-Hustle
Rollover from previous week		☐	☐	☐	☐
		☐	☐	☐	☐
		☐	☐	☐	☐
		☐	☐	☐	☐
		☐	☐	☐	☐
		☐	☐	☐	☐
		☐	☐	☐	☐
		☐	☐	☐	☐
		☐	☐	☐	☐
Total Income	$				
minus - Total Cash Envelopes	$				
Remaining Balance	$				

Double Check It! Calculations

Cash Breakdown

Date:

CASH ENVELOPES/SINKING FUNDS

CATEGORY	AMOUNT	BANKING WITHDRAWAL DENOMINATIONS					
		$1	$5	$10	$20	$50	$100
		Total Number of Each Bill					
TOTAL	$						

INCOME

INCOME SOURCE	AMOUNT	Salary/Wages	Investment	Business	Side-Hustle
Rollover from previous week		☐	☐	☐	☐
		☐	☐	☐	☐
		☐	☐	☐	☐
		☐	☐	☐	☐
		☐	☐	☐	☐
		☐	☐	☐	☐
		☐	☐	☐	☐
		☐	☐	☐	☐
		☐	☐	☐	☐

Total Income	$
minus - Total Cash Envelopes	$
Remaining Balance	$

Double Check It! Calculations

Cash Breakdown

Date:

CASH ENVELOPES/SINKING FUNDS

CATEGORY	AMOUNT	BANKING WITHDRAWAL DENOMINATIONS					
		$1	$5	$10	$20	$50	$100
		Total Number of Each Bill					
TOTAL	$						

INCOME

INCOME SOURCE	AMOUNT	Salary/Wages	Investment	Business	Side-Hustle
Rollover from previous week		☐	☐	☐	☐
		☐	☐	☐	☐
		☐	☐	☐	☐
		☐	☐	☐	☐
		☐	☐	☐	☐
		☐	☐	☐	☐
		☐	☐	☐	☐
		☐	☐	☐	☐
		☐	☐	☐	☐
Total Income	$				
minus - Total Cash Envelopes	$				
Remaining Balance	$				

Double Check It! Calculations

Cash Breakdown

Date:

CASH ENVELOPES/SINKING FUNDS

CATEGORY	AMOUNT	BANKING WITHDRAWAL DENOMINATIONS					
		$1	$5	$10	$20	$50	$100
		Total Number of Each Bill					
TOTAL	$						

INCOME

INCOME SOURCE	AMOUNT	Salary/Wages	Investment	Business	Side-Hustle
Rollover from previous week		☐	☐	☐	☐
		☐	☐	☐	☐
		☐	☐	☐	☐
		☐	☐	☐	☐
		☐	☐	☐	☐
		☐	☐	☐	☐
		☐	☐	☐	☐
		☐	☐	☐	☐
		☐	☐	☐	☐
Total Income	$				
minus - Total Cash Envelopes	$				
Remaining Balance	$				

Double Check It! Calculations

Cash Breakdown

Date:

CASH ENVELOPES/SINKING FUNDS

CATEGORY	AMOUNT	BANKING WITHDRAWAL DENOMINATIONS					
		$1	$5	$10	$20	$50	$100
		Total Number of Each Bill					
TOTAL	$						

INCOME

INCOME SOURCE	AMOUNT	Salary/Wages	Investment	Business	Side-Hustle
Rollover from previous week		☐	☐	☐	☐
		☐	☐	☐	☐
		☐	☐	☐	☐
		☐	☐	☐	☐
		☐	☐	☐	☐
		☐	☐	☐	☐
		☐	☐	☐	☐
		☐	☐	☐	☐
		☐	☐	☐	☐
Total Income	$				
minus - Total Cash Envelopes	$				
Remaining Balance	$				

Double Check It! Calculations

Cash Breakdown

Date:

CASH ENVELOPES/SINKING FUNDS

CATEGORY	AMOUNT	BANKING WITHDRAWAL DENOMINATIONS					
		$1	$5	$10	$20	$50	$100
		Total Number of Each Bill					
TOTAL	$						

INCOME

INCOME SOURCE	AMOUNT	Salary/Wages	Investment	Business	Side-Hustle
Rollover from previous week		☐	☐	☐	☐
		☐	☐	☐	☐
		☐	☐	☐	☐
		☐	☐	☐	☐
		☐	☐	☐	☐
		☐	☐	☐	☐
		☐	☐	☐	☐
		☐	☐	☐	☐
		☐	☐	☐	☐
Total Income	$				
minus - Total Cash Envelopes	$				
Remaining Balance	$				

Double Check It! Calculations

Cash Breakdown

Date:

CASH ENVELOPES/SINKING FUNDS

CATEGORY	AMOUNT	BANKING WITHDRAWAL DENOMINATIONS					
		$1	$5	$10	$20	$50	$100
		Total Number of Each Bill					
TOTAL	$						

INCOME

INCOME SOURCE	AMOUNT	Salary/Wages	Investment	Business	Side-Hustle
Rollover from previous week		☐	☐	☐	☐
		☐	☐	☐	☐
		☐	☐	☐	☐
		☐	☐	☐	☐
		☐	☐	☐	☐
		☐	☐	☐	☐
		☐	☐	☐	☐
		☐	☐	☐	☐
		☐	☐	☐	☐
Total Income	$				
minus - Total Cash Envelopes	$				
Remaining Balance	$				

Double Check It! Calculations

Cash Breakdown

Date:

CASH ENVELOPES/SINKING FUNDS

CATEGORY	AMOUNT	BANKING WITHDRAWAL DENOMINATIONS					
		$1	$5	$10	$20	$50	$100
		Total Number of Each Bill					
TOTAL	$						

INCOME

INCOME SOURCE	AMOUNT	Salary/Wages	Investment	Business	Side-Hustle
Rollover from previous week		☐	☐	☐	☐
		☐	☐	☐	☐
		☐	☐	☐	☐
		☐	☐	☐	☐
		☐	☐	☐	☐
		☐	☐	☐	☐
		☐	☐	☐	☐
		☐	☐	☐	☐
		☐	☐	☐	☐
Total Income	$				
minus - Total Cash Envelopes	$				
Remaining Balance	$				

Double Check It! Calculations

Cash Breakdown

Date:

CASH ENVELOPES/SINKING FUNDS

CATEGORY	AMOUNT	BANKING WITHDRAWAL DENOMINATIONS					
		$1	$5	$10	$20	$50	$100
		Total Number of Each Bill					
TOTAL	$						

INCOME

INCOME SOURCE	AMOUNT	Salary/Wages	Investment	Business	Side-Hustle
Rollover from previous week		☐	☐	☐	☐
		☐	☐	☐	☐
		☐	☐	☐	☐
		☐	☐	☐	☐
		☐	☐	☐	☐
		☐	☐	☐	☐
		☐	☐	☐	☐
		☐	☐	☐	☐
		☐	☐	☐	☐
Total Income	$				
minus - Total Cash Envelopes	$				
Remaining Balance	$				

Double Check It! Calculations

Cash Breakdown

Date:

CASH ENVELOPES/SINKING FUNDS

CATEGORY	AMOUNT	BANKING WITHDRAWAL DENOMINATIONS					
		$1	$5	$10	$20	$50	$100
		Total Number of Each Bill					
TOTAL	$						

INCOME

INCOME SOURCE	AMOUNT	Salary/Wages	Investment	Business	Side-Hustle
Rollover from previous week		☐	☐	☐	☐
		☐	☐	☐	☐
		☐	☐	☐	☐
		☐	☐	☐	☐
		☐	☐	☐	☐
		☐	☐	☐	☐
		☐	☐	☐	☐
		☐	☐	☐	☐
		☐	☐	☐	☐
Total Income	$				
minus - Total Cash Envelopes	$				
Remaining Balance	$				

Double Check It! Calculations

Cash Breakdown

Date:

CASH ENVELOPES/SINKING FUNDS

CATEGORY	AMOUNT	BANKING WITHDRAWAL DENOMINATIONS					
		$1	$5	$10	$20	$50	$100
		Total Number of Each Bill					
TOTAL	$						

INCOME

INCOME SOURCE	AMOUNT	Salary/Wages	Investment	Business	Side-Hustle
Rollover from previous week		☐	☐	☐	☐
		☐	☐	☐	☐
		☐	☐	☐	☐
		☐	☐	☐	☐
		☐	☐	☐	☐
		☐	☐	☐	☐
		☐	☐	☐	☐
		☐	☐	☐	☐
		☐	☐	☐	☐
Total Income	$				
minus - Total Cash Envelopes	$				
Remaining Balance	$				

Double Check It! Calculations

Cash Breakdown

Date:

CASH ENVELOPES/SINKING FUNDS

CATEGORY	AMOUNT	BANKING WITHDRAWAL DENOMINATIONS					
		$1	$5	$10	$20	$50	$100
		Total Number of Each Bill					
TOTAL	$						

INCOME

INCOME SOURCE	AMOUNT	Salary/Wages	Investment	Business	Side-Hustle
Rollover from previous week		☐	☐	☐	☐
		☐	☐	☐	☐
		☐	☐	☐	☐
		☐	☐	☐	☐
		☐	☐	☐	☐
		☐	☐	☐	☐
		☐	☐	☐	☐
		☐	☐	☐	☐
		☐	☐	☐	☐
Total Income	$				
minus - Total Cash Envelopes	$				
Remaining Balance	$				

Double Check It! Calculations

Cash Breakdown

Date:

CASH ENVELOPES/SINKING FUNDS

CATEGORY	AMOUNT	BANKING WITHDRAWAL DENOMINATIONS					
		$1	$5	$10	$20	$50	$100
		Total Number of Each Bill					
TOTAL	$						

INCOME

INCOME SOURCE	AMOUNT	Salary/Wages	Investment	Business	Side-Hustle
Rollover from previous week		☐	☐	☐	☐
		☐	☐	☐	☐
		☐	☐	☐	☐
		☐	☐	☐	☐
		☐	☐	☐	☐
		☐	☐	☐	☐
		☐	☐	☐	☐
		☐	☐	☐	☐
		☐	☐	☐	☐
Total Income	$				
minus - Total Cash Envelopes	$				
Remaining Balance	$				

Double Check It! Calculations

Cash Breakdown

Date:

CASH ENVELOPES/SINKING FUNDS

CATEGORY	AMOUNT	BANKING WITHDRAWAL DENOMINATIONS					
		$1	$5	$10	$20	$50	$100
		Total Number of Each Bill					
TOTAL	$						

INCOME

INCOME SOURCE	AMOUNT	Salary/Wages	Investment	Business	Side-Hustle
Rollover from previous week		☐	☐	☐	☐
		☐	☐	☐	☐
		☐	☐	☐	☐
		☐	☐	☐	☐
		☐	☐	☐	☐
		☐	☐	☐	☐
		☐	☐	☐	☐
		☐	☐	☐	☐
		☐	☐	☐	☐
Total Income	$				
minus - Total Cash Envelopes	$				
Remaining Balance	$				

Double Check It! Calculations

Cash Breakdown

Date:

CASH ENVELOPES/SINKING FUNDS

CATEGORY	AMOUNT	BANKING WITHDRAWAL DENOMINATIONS					
		$1	$5	$10	$20	$50	$100
		Total Number of Each Bill					
TOTAL	$						

INCOME

INCOME SOURCE	AMOUNT	Salary/Wages	Investment	Business	Side-Hustle
Rollover from previous week		☐	☐	☐	☐
		☐	☐	☐	☐
		☐	☐	☐	☐
		☐	☐	☐	☐
		☐	☐	☐	☐
		☐	☐	☐	☐
		☐	☐	☐	☐
		☐	☐	☐	☐
		☐	☐	☐	☐
Total Income	$				
minus - Total Cash Envelopes	$				
Remaining Balance	$				

Double Check It! Calculations

Cash Breakdown

Date:

CASH ENVELOPES/SINKING FUNDS

CATEGORY	AMOUNT	BANKING WITHDRAWAL DENOMINATIONS					
		$1	$5	$10	$20	$50	$100
		Total Number of Each Bill					
TOTAL	$						

INCOME

INCOME SOURCE	AMOUNT	Salary/Wages	Investment	Business	Side-Hustle
Rollover from previous week		☐	☐	☐	☐
		☐	☐	☐	☐
		☐	☐	☐	☐
		☐	☐	☐	☐
		☐	☐	☐	☐
		☐	☐	☐	☐
		☐	☐	☐	☐
		☐	☐	☐	☐
		☐	☐	☐	☐
Total Income	$				
minus - Total Cash Envelopes	$				
Remaining Balance	$				

Double Check It! Calculations

Cash Breakdown

Date:

CASH ENVELOPES/SINKING FUNDS

CATEGORY	AMOUNT	BANKING WITHDRAWAL DENOMINATIONS					
		$1	$5	$10	$20	$50	$100
		Total Number of Each Bill					
TOTAL	$						

INCOME

INCOME SOURCE	AMOUNT	Salary/Wages	Investment	Business	Side-Hustle
Rollover from previous week		☐	☐	☐	☐
		☐	☐	☐	☐
		☐	☐	☐	☐
		☐	☐	☐	☐
		☐	☐	☐	☐
		☐	☐	☐	☐
		☐	☐	☐	☐
		☐	☐	☐	☐
		☐	☐	☐	☐
Total Income	$				
minus - Total Cash Envelopes	$				
Remaining Balance	$				

Double Check It! Calculations

Cash Breakdown

Date:

CASH ENVELOPES/SINKING FUNDS

CATEGORY	AMOUNT	BANKING WITHDRAWAL DENOMINATIONS					
		$1	$5	$10	$20	$50	$100
		Total Number of Each Bill					
TOTAL	$						

INCOME

INCOME SOURCE	AMOUNT	Salary/Wages	Investment	Business	Side-Hustle
Rollover from previous week		☐	☐	☐	☐
		☐	☐	☐	☐
		☐	☐	☐	☐
		☐	☐	☐	☐
		☐	☐	☐	☐
		☐	☐	☐	☐
		☐	☐	☐	☐
		☐	☐	☐	☐
		☐	☐	☐	☐
Total Income	$				
minus - Total Cash Envelopes	$				
Remaining Balance	$				

Double Check It! Calculations

Made in the USA
Las Vegas, NV
03 November 2026

57421980R00038